VISUAL ELEMENTS 1

PICTOGRAMS

VISUAL ELEMENTS 1

ROCKPORT PUBLISHERS • ROCKPORT, MASSACHUSETTS

Distributed by North Light Books • Cincinnati, Ohio

Distributed to the book trade and art trade in
the U.S. and Canada by:
North Light, an imprint of
Writer's Digest Books
1507 Dana Avenue
Cincinnati, Ohio 45207
(513) 985-0717

First published in Great Britain in 1989 by:
Columbus Books, Ltd.
19-23 Ludgate Hill
London EC4M 7PD
ISBN: 0-86287 955 8
Price: £11.95

Other distribution by:
Rockport Publishers, Inc.
5 Smith Street
Rockport, Massachusetts 01966
(508) 546-9590
Telex: 5106019284
Fax: (508) 546-7141
ISBN: 0-935603-15-8

First published in Japan. First English
language edition published by Rockport
Publishers.

Visual Elements 1: Pictograms was
produced by:
Blount & Company
Number Twelve Station Road
Cranbury, New Jersey 08512
(609) 655-5785

Printed in the United States

CONTENTS

Cherry	89	Watermelon	89	Swimming	66
Cocks comb	91	Wheat	90	Tennis	58, 65
Corn	90			Third baseman	57
Cosmos	91			Volleyball	60, 65
Cucumber	88, 90			Wind surfing	66

Sports

Miscellaneous

Dahlia	91	Archery	62		
Daikon radish	88, 90	Badminton	59	Art	119
Eggplant	88, 90	Baseball	65	Ballet	117
Freesia	91	Basketball	60	Bath	116
Fringed pink	91	Batter	57	Barber	104
Gentian	87, 91	Bowling	61	Big Ben (London)	108
Gladiolus	87	Boxing	65	Biology	119
Grapes	89	Canoe	66	Bolt	119
Green onion	88, 90	Catcher	57	Boot	116
Hibiscus	91	Cycling	64	Bowl	114
Hyacinth	86	Diving	63	Brasilia National Conference Hall	106
Iris	86	First baseman	57	Chemistry	119
Lily	86, 91	Fishing	63, 66	Chinese cuisine	114
Loquat	89	Flying ring	65	Clock	109
Melon	89	Frisbee	62	Coffee	114
Mum	88	Football	65	Comb, scissors	115
Orchid	87, 91	Golf	61, 66	Condominium	104
Peach	89	Hang gliding	65	Construction	110
Pear	89	Hockey	61	Cooking	116
Peas	88	Ice hockey	66	Cooking oil	112
Pineapple	89	Jogging	62, 64	Cooking pot	116
Potato	88	Judo	66	Cosmetics	116
Primrose	86	Marathon	65	Cupid	117
Pumpkin	88, 90	Motor cross	66	Documentary	117
Rape-blossoms	86	Pitcher	57	Drafting	111
Rhododendron	87	Poses	62, 64	Drinks	116
Rice	90	Road Racing	61	Drive	116
Rose	91	Roller Skating	62, 65	Economics	119
Shiitake mushroom	90	Rugby	61, 65	Eggplant	116
Strawberry	89	Scuba diving	63, 66	Electronic scale	120
Sweet potato	88	Second baseman	57	English	119
Sunflower	87	Skate	66	Entertainment	111
Tangerine	89	Skiing	62, 64, 66	Factory	110
Thistle	91	Soccer	61, 65	Fan	120
Tomato	88	Sumo	66		
		Surfing	63		

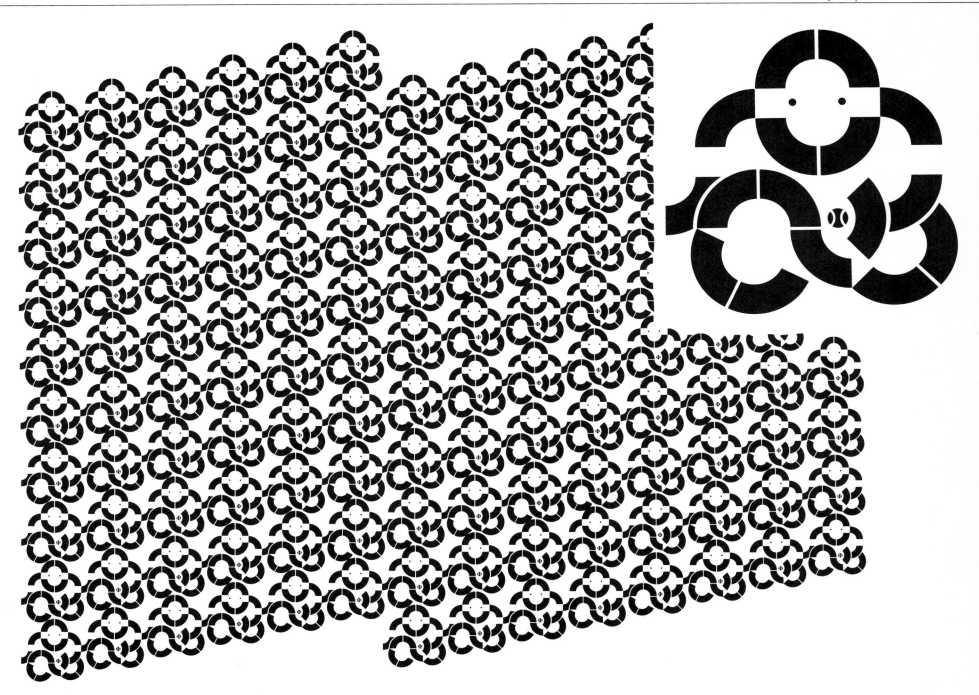

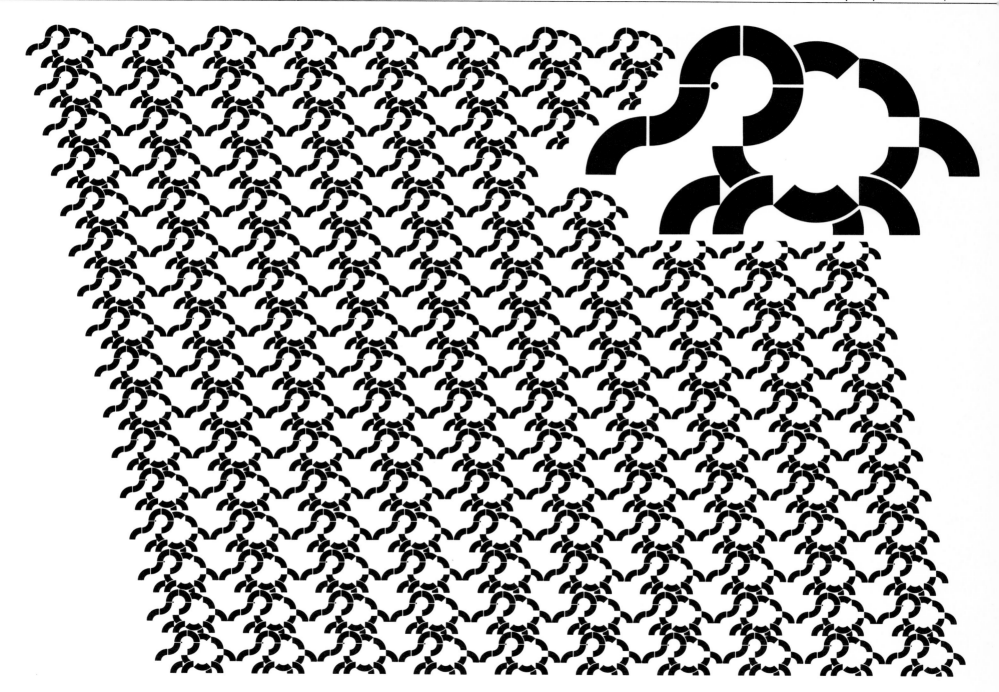

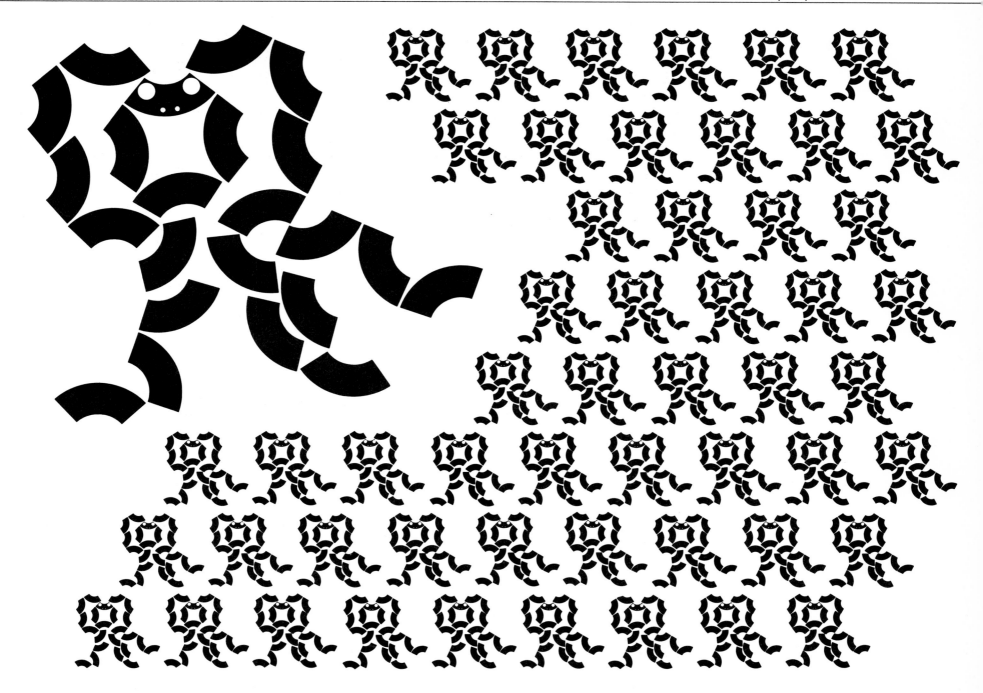

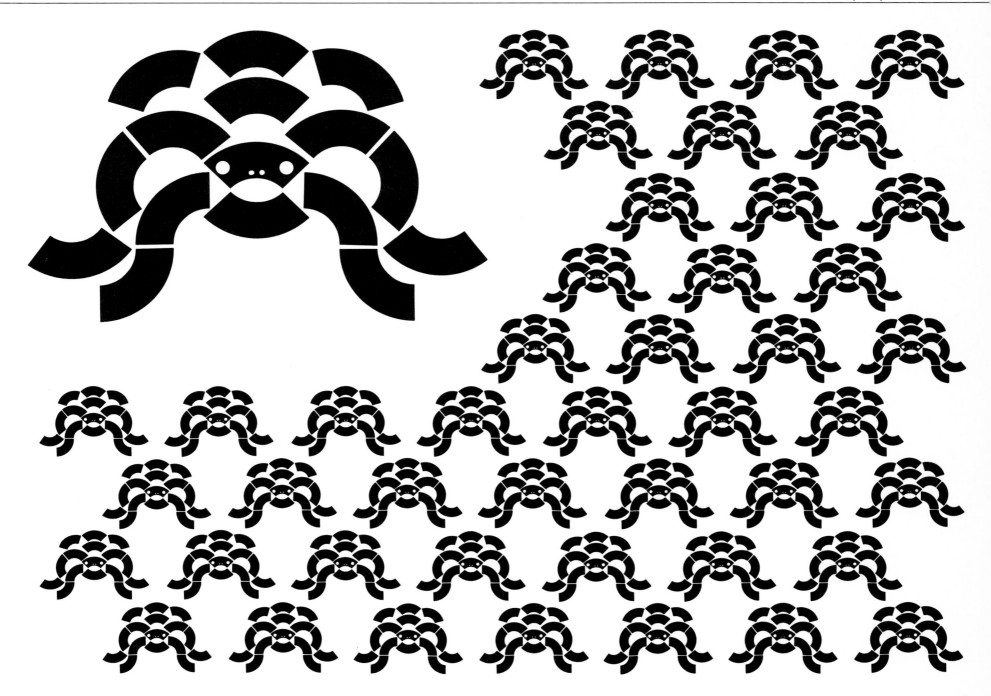

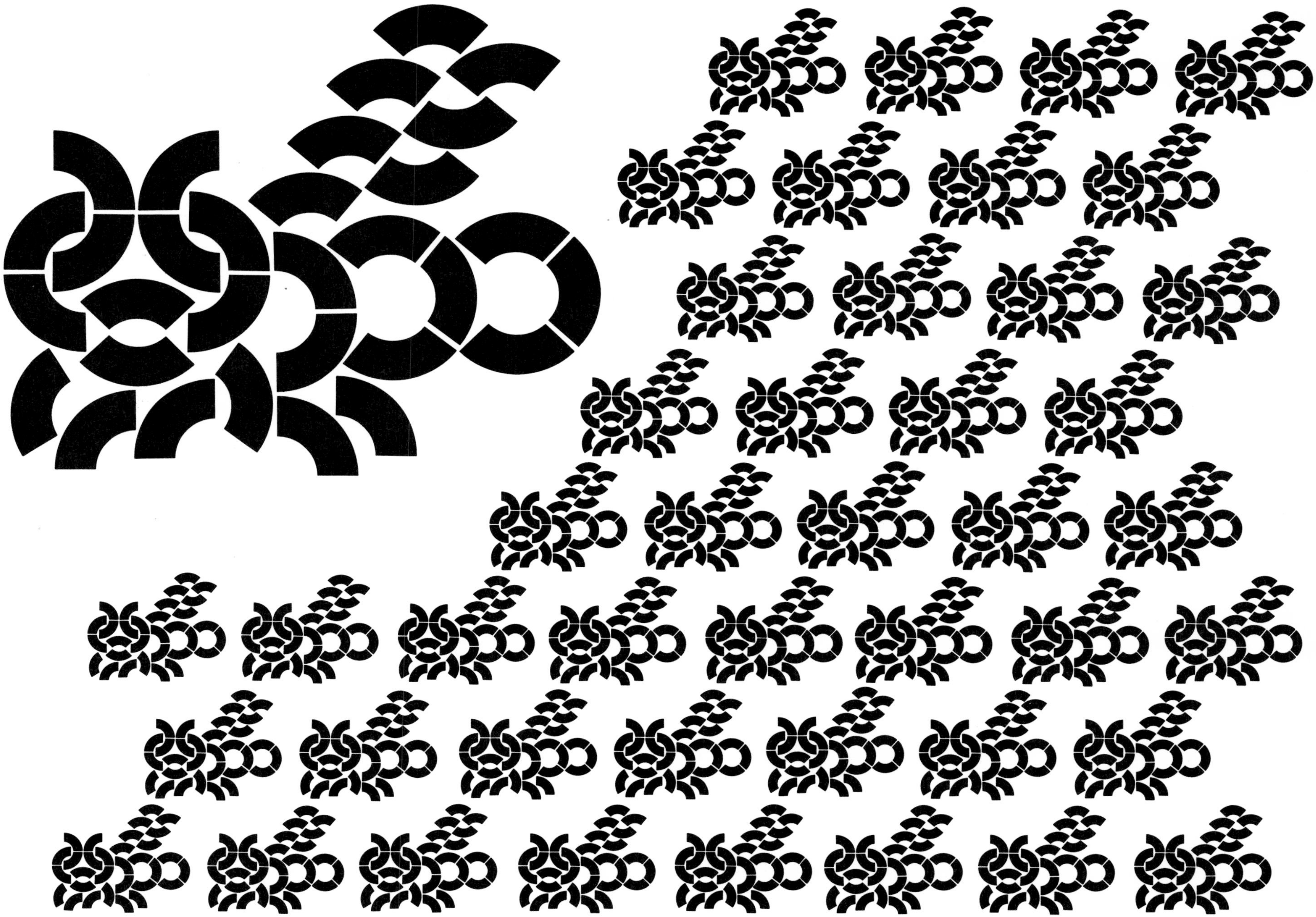

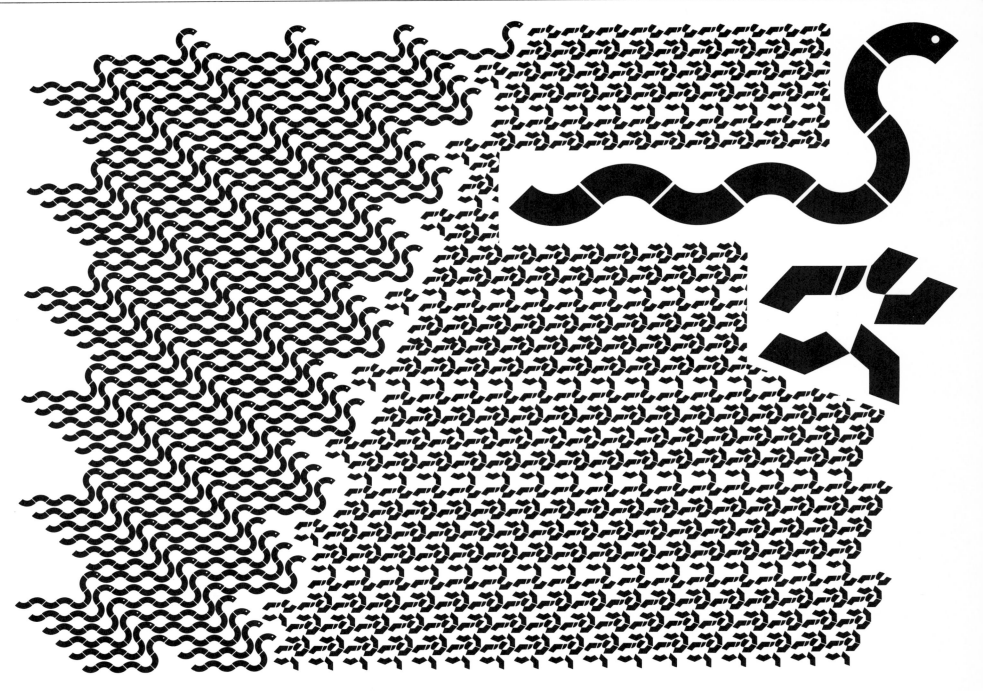

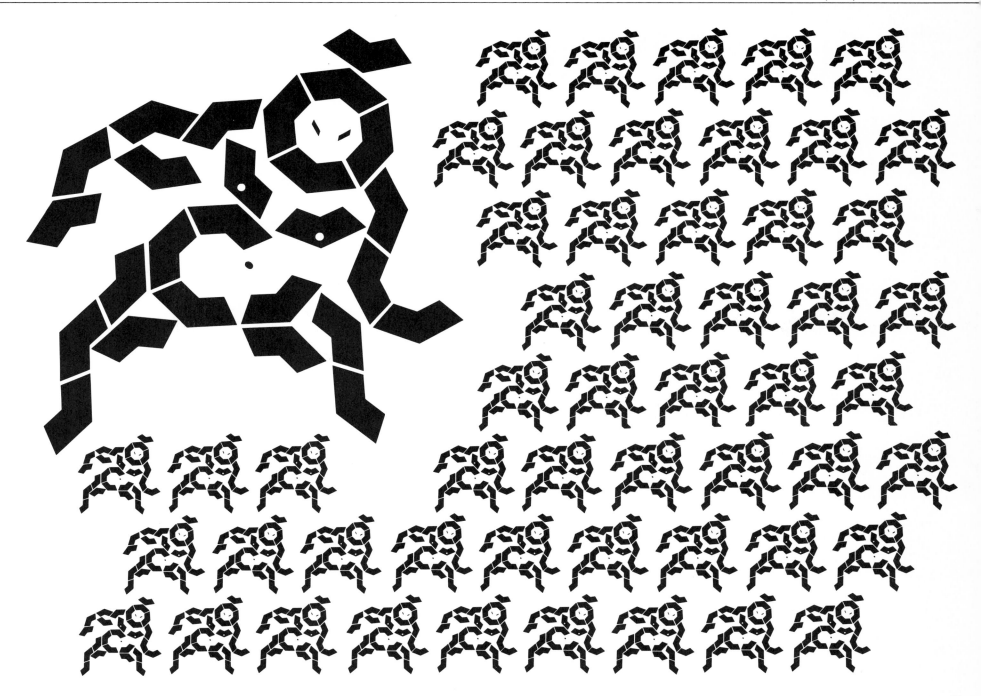

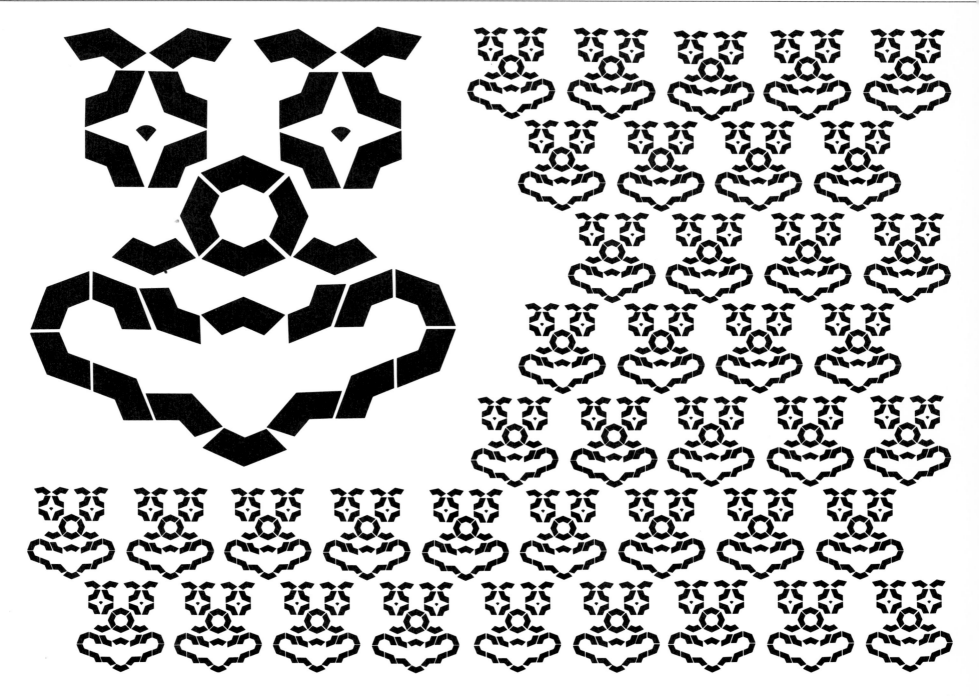

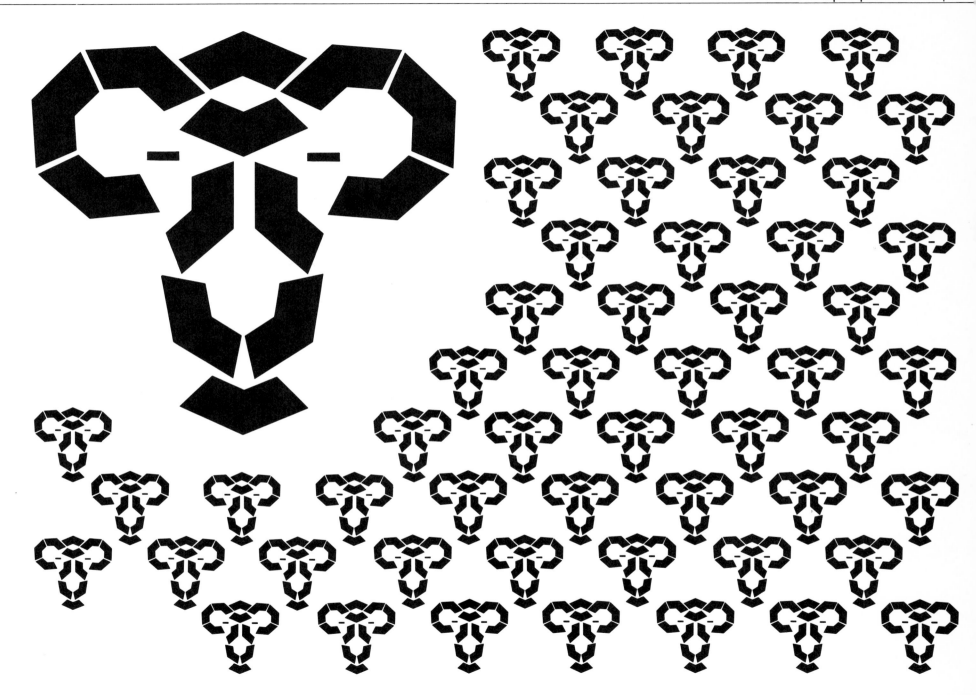

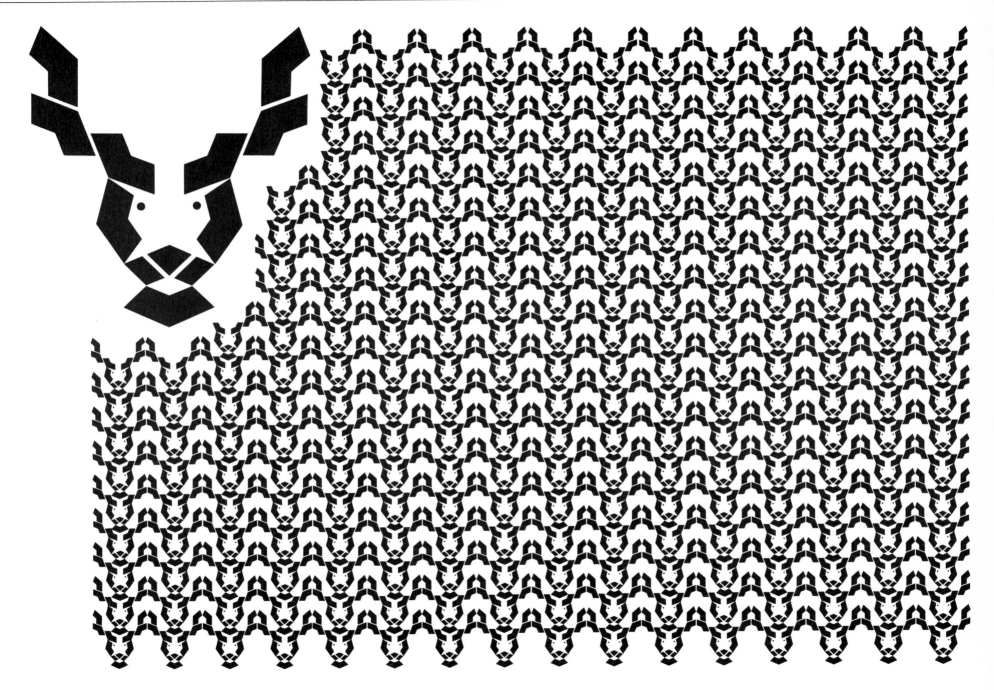

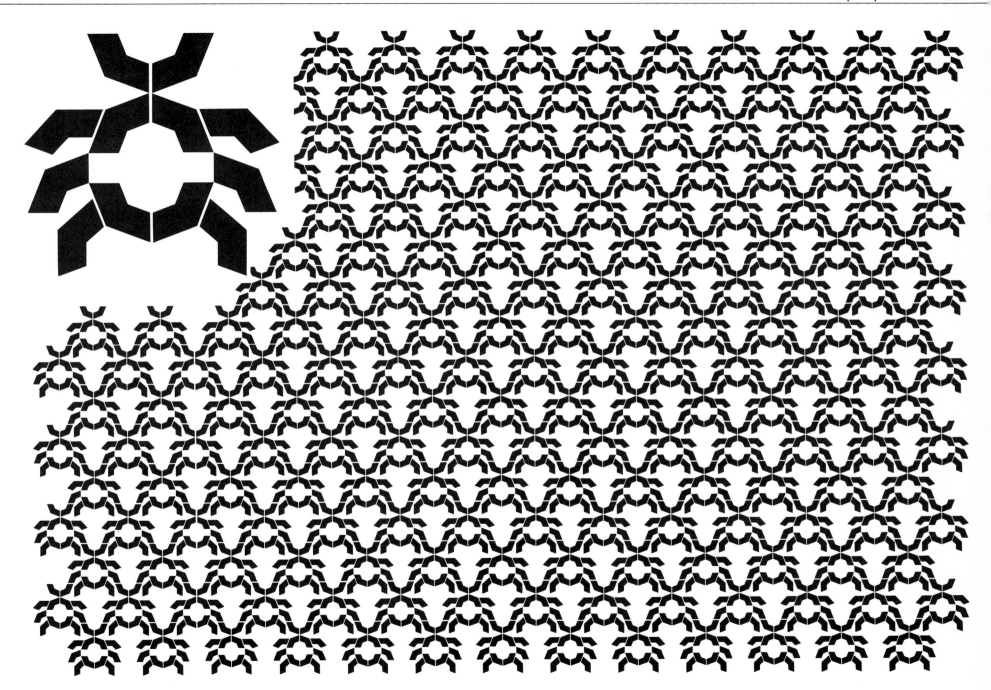

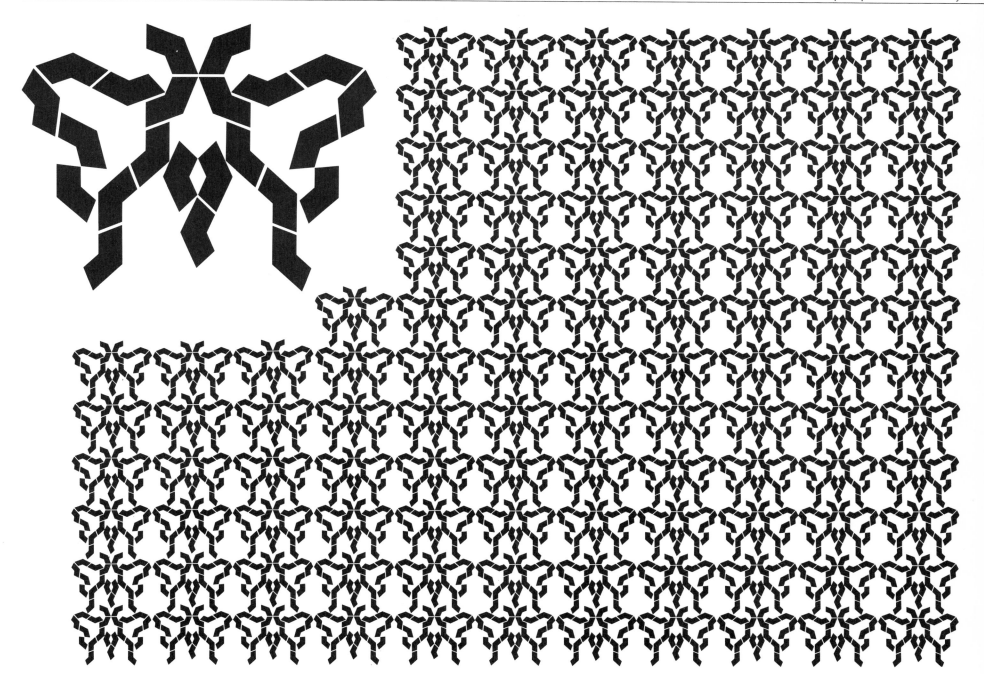

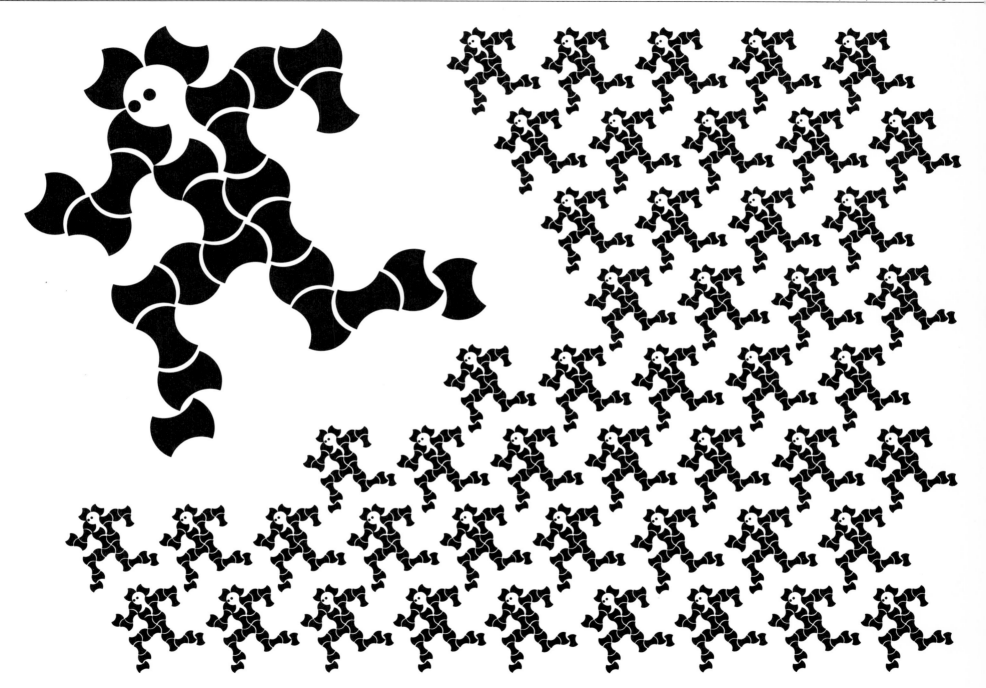

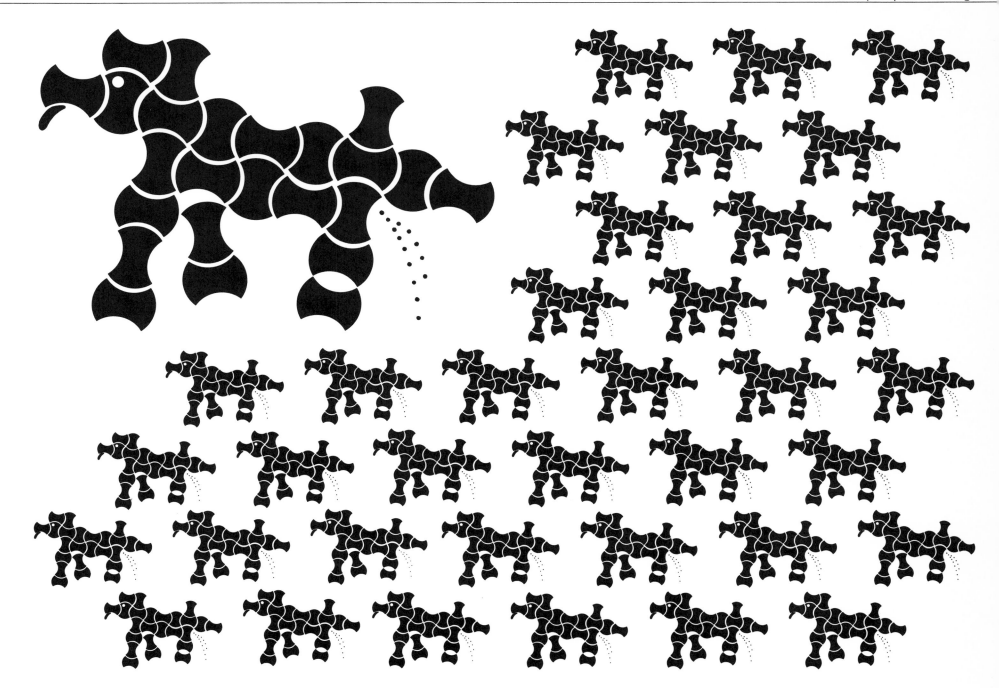

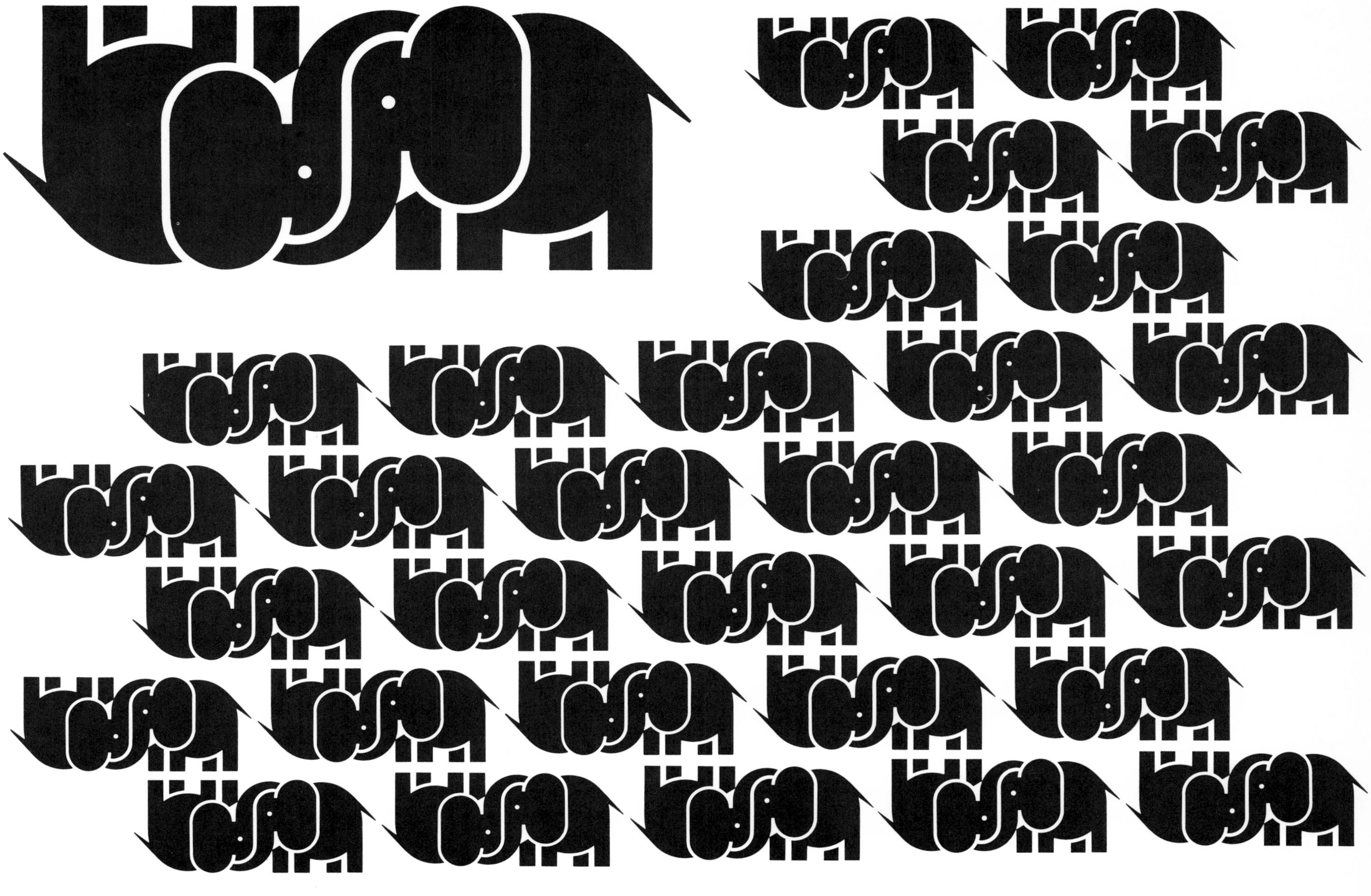

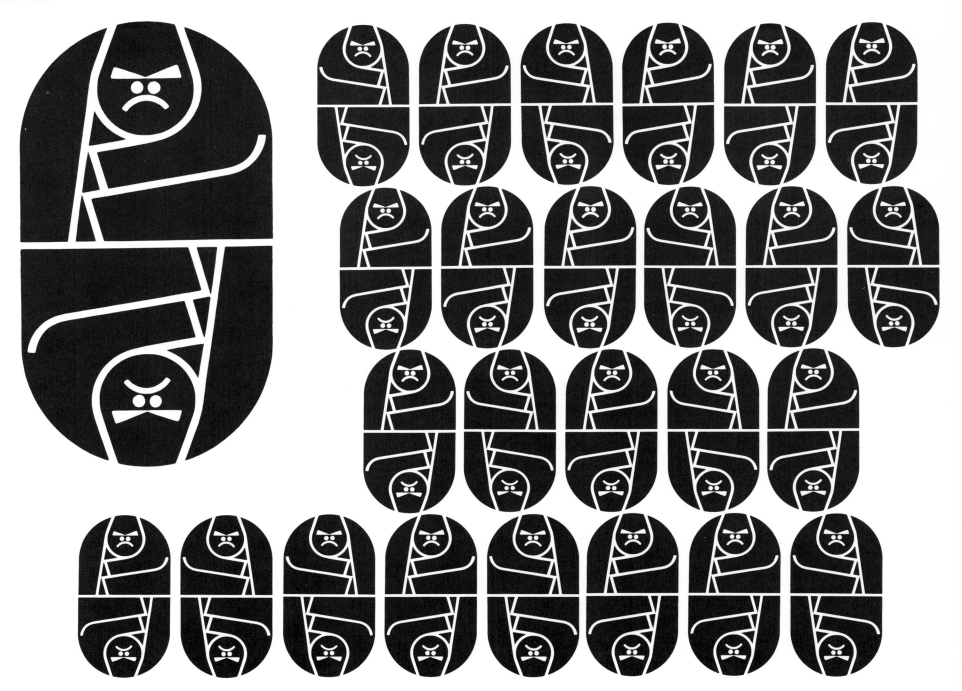

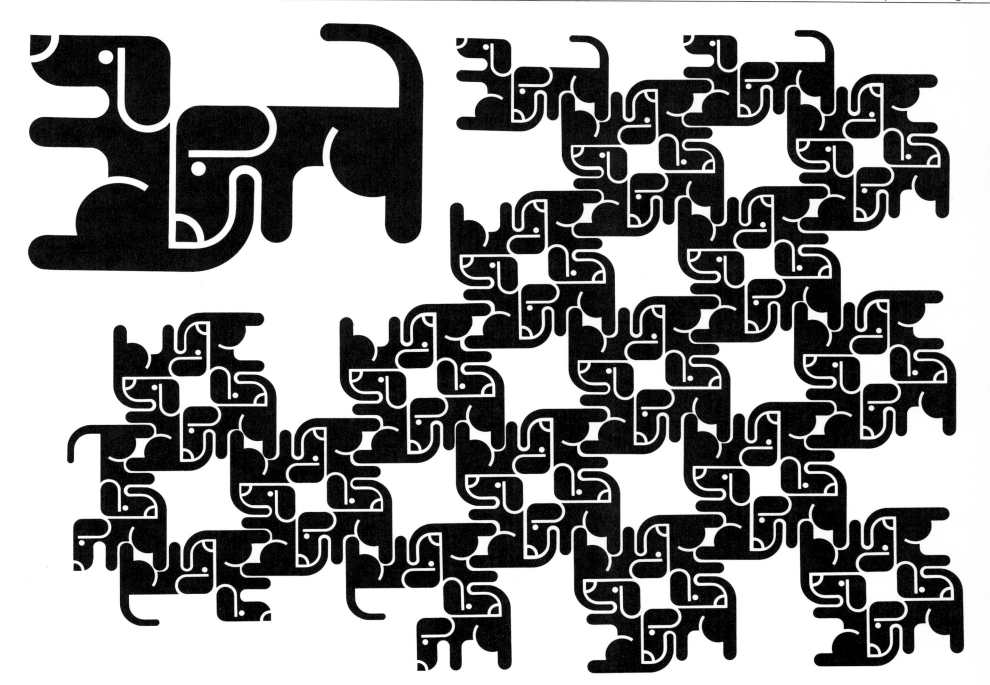

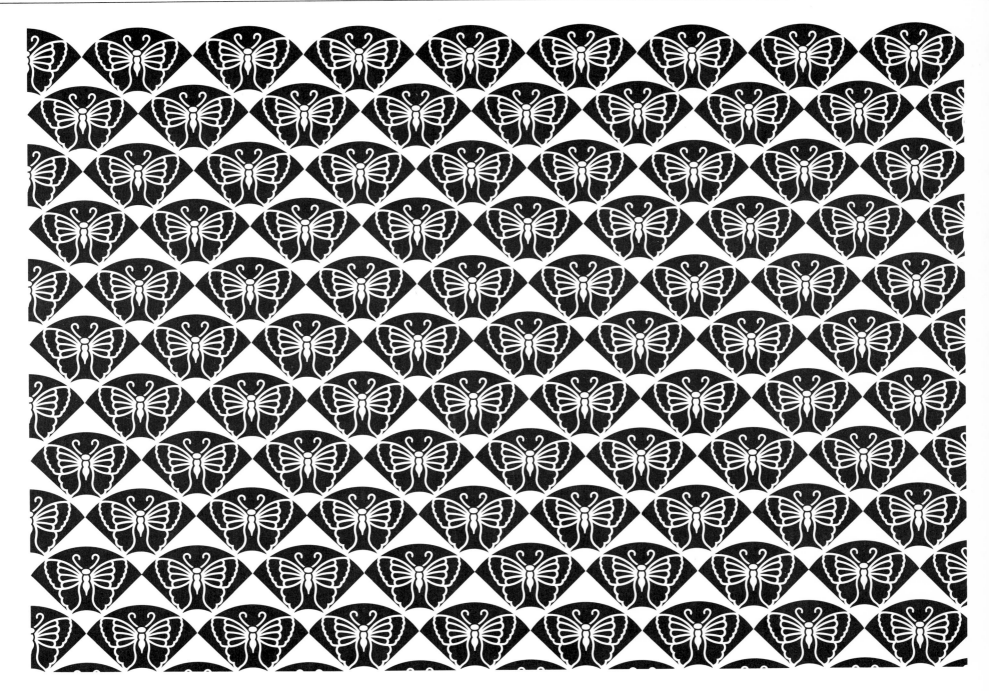

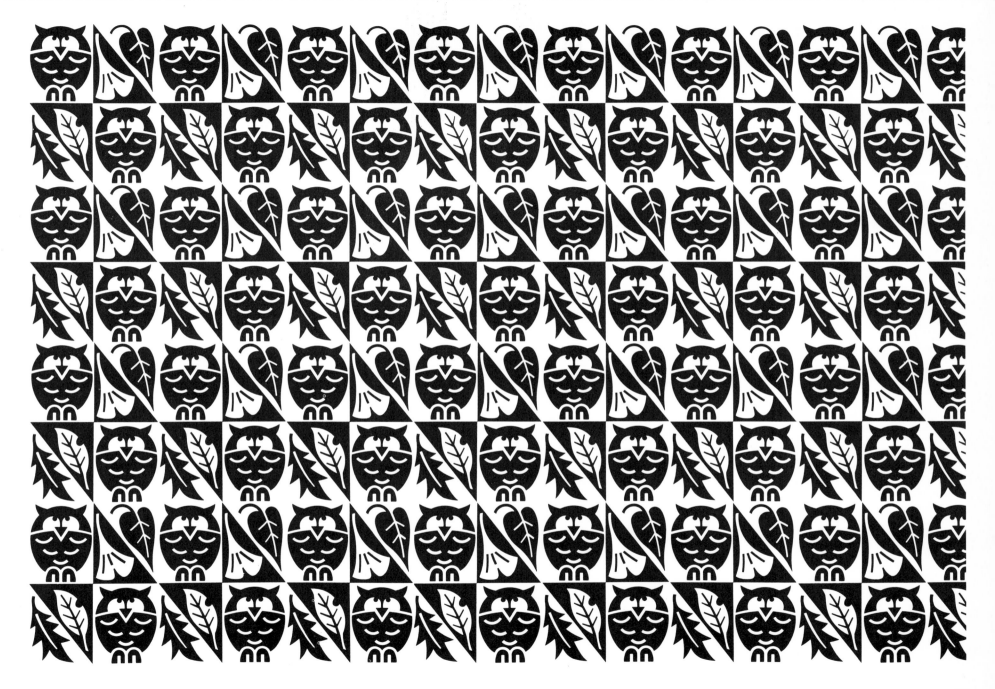

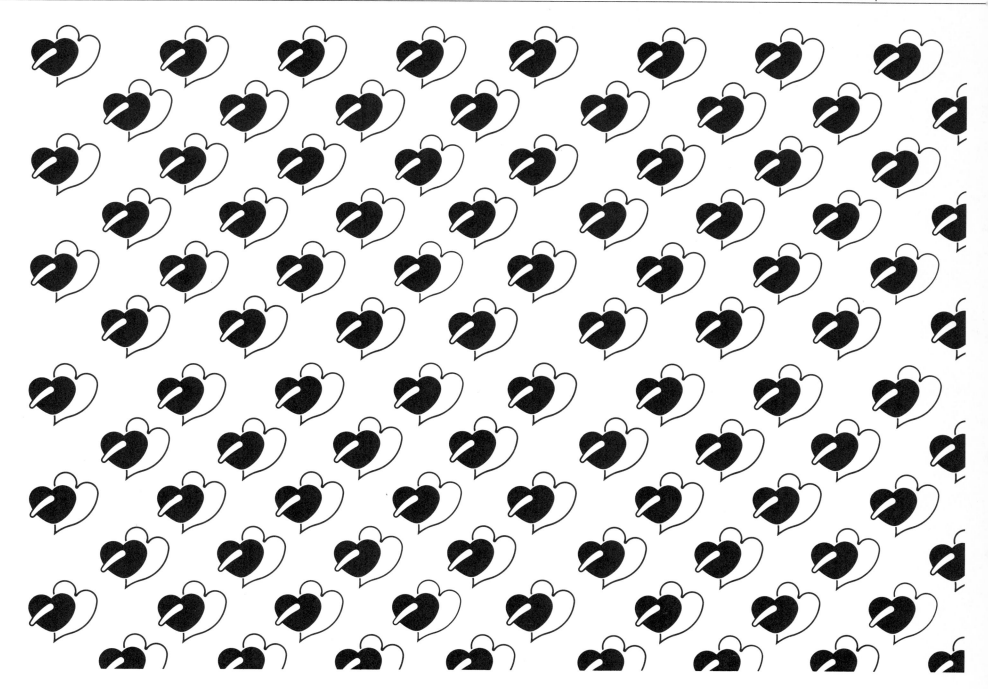

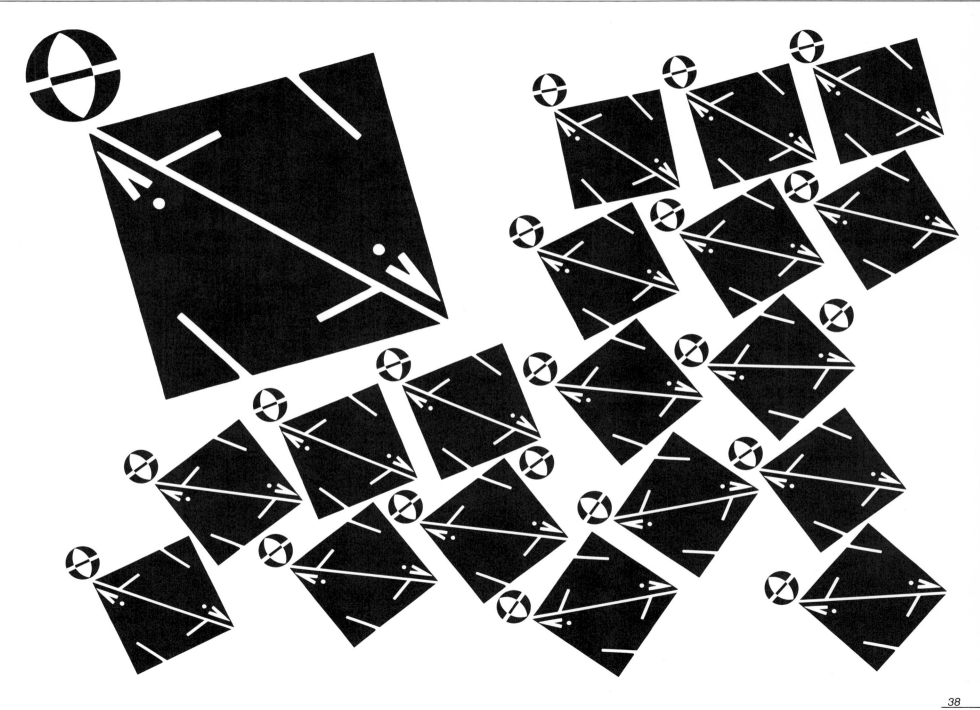

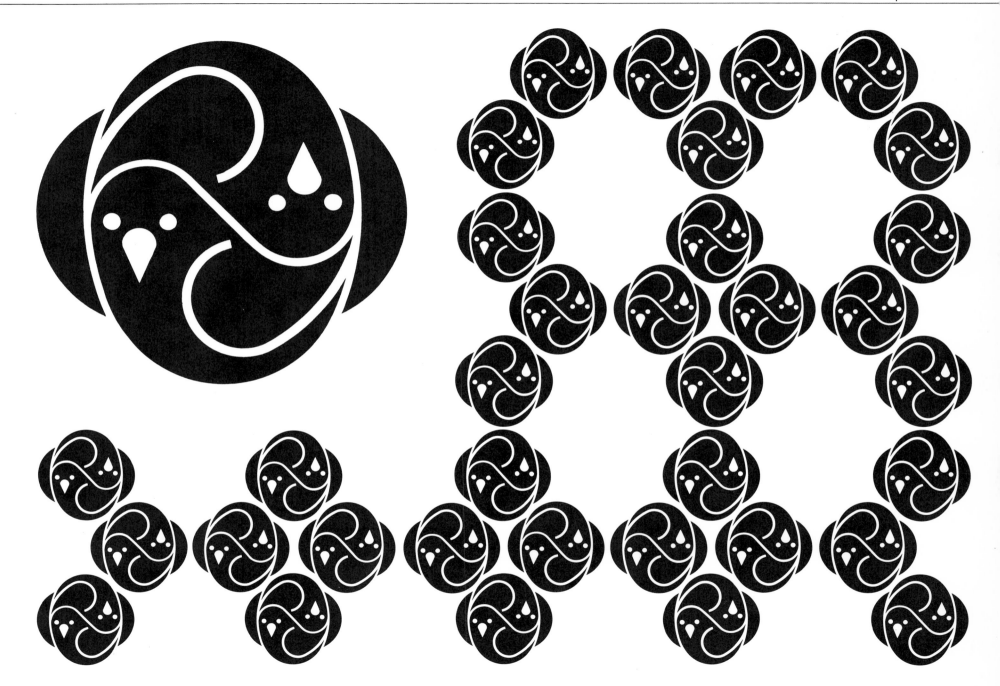

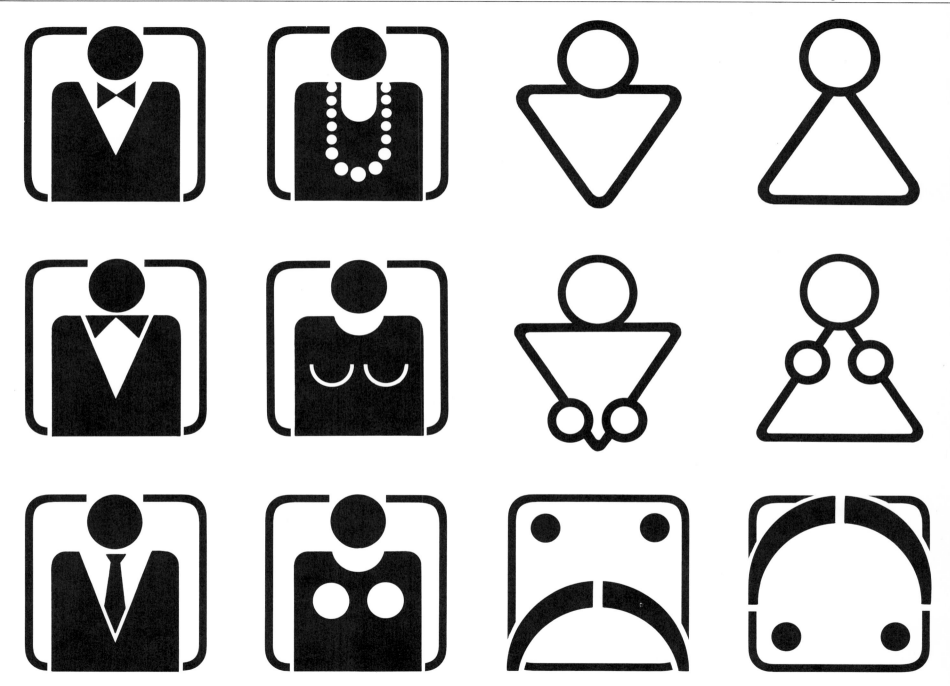

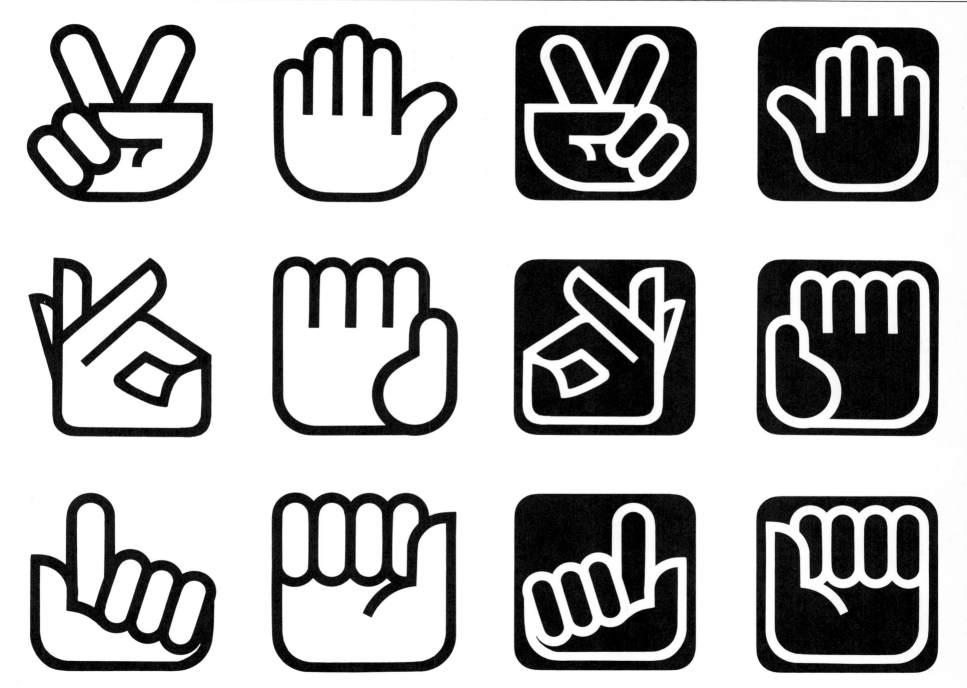

1

2

3

4

5

6

7

8

9

10

11

12

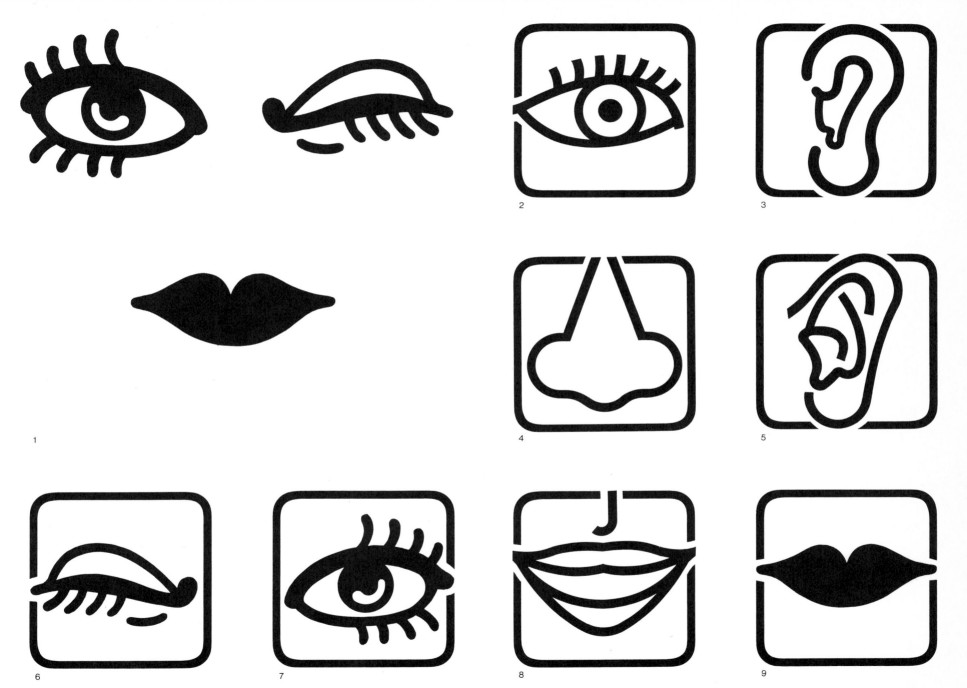

1

2

3

4

5

6

7

8

9

1

2

3

4

5

6

7

8

9

10

11

12

13

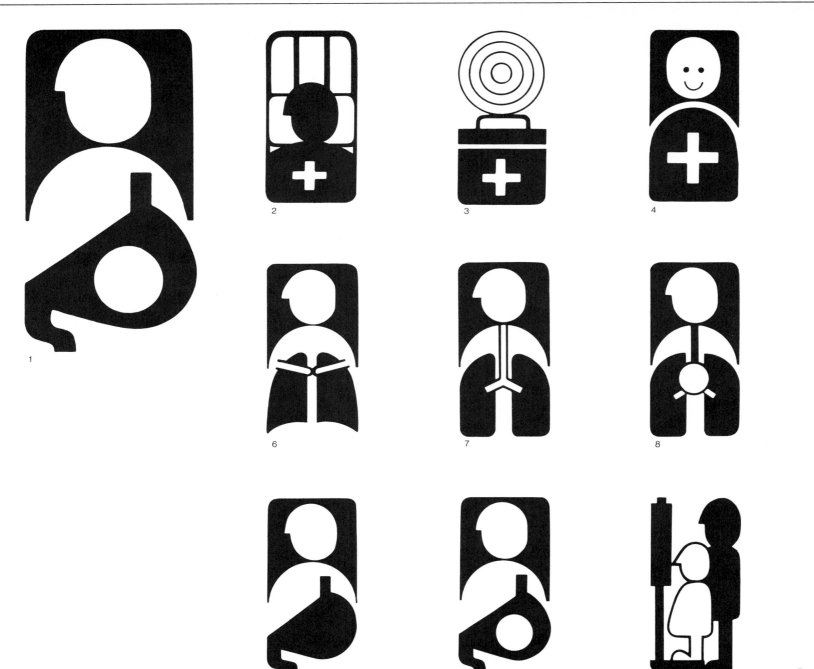

1

2

3

4

5

6

7

8

9

10

11

12

1

2

3

4

5

6

7

8

9

10

11

12

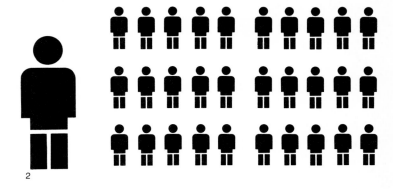

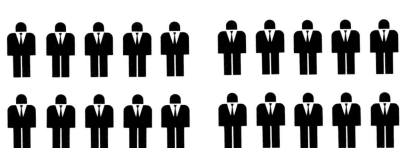

1

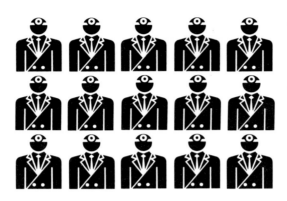

2

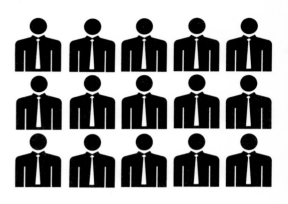

3

4

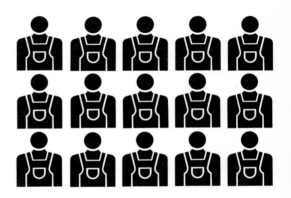

5

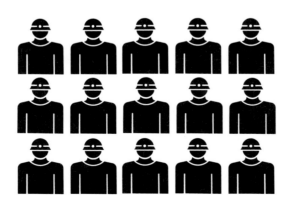

6

1

2

3

4

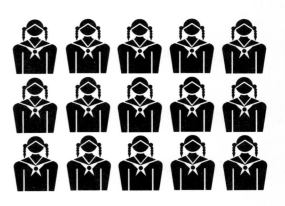

5

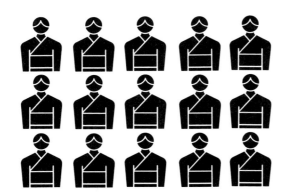

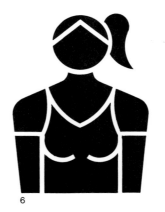

6

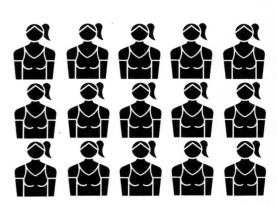

1

2

3

4

5

6

7

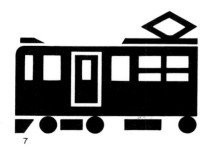

8

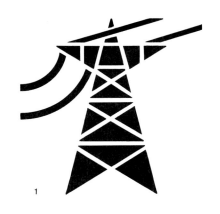

1

2

3

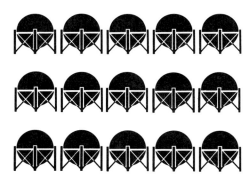

4

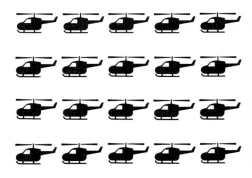

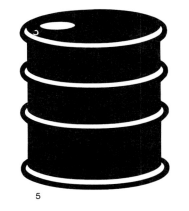

5

6

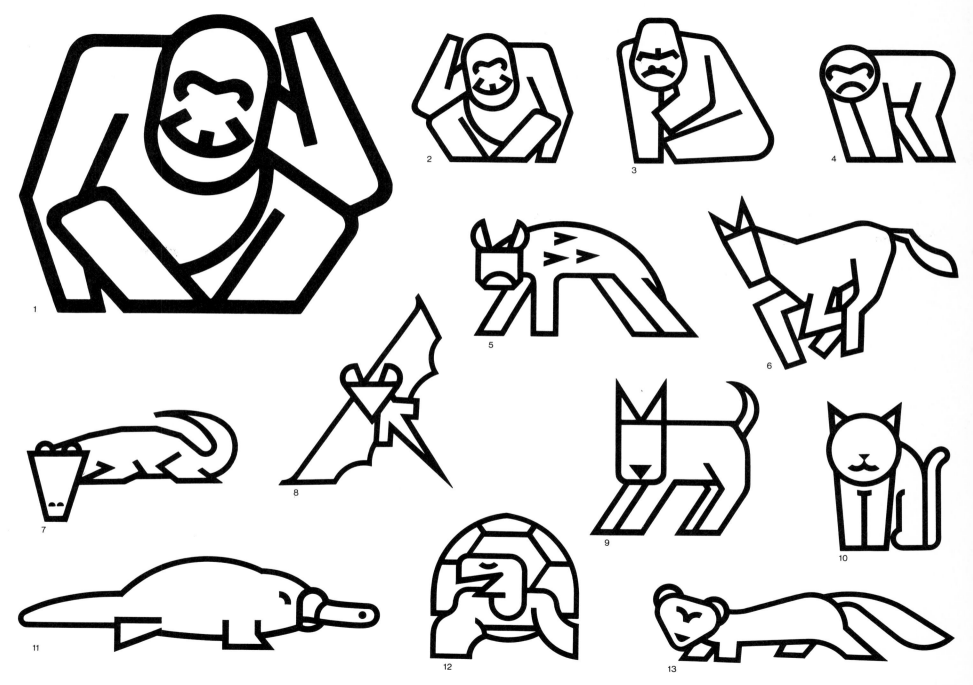

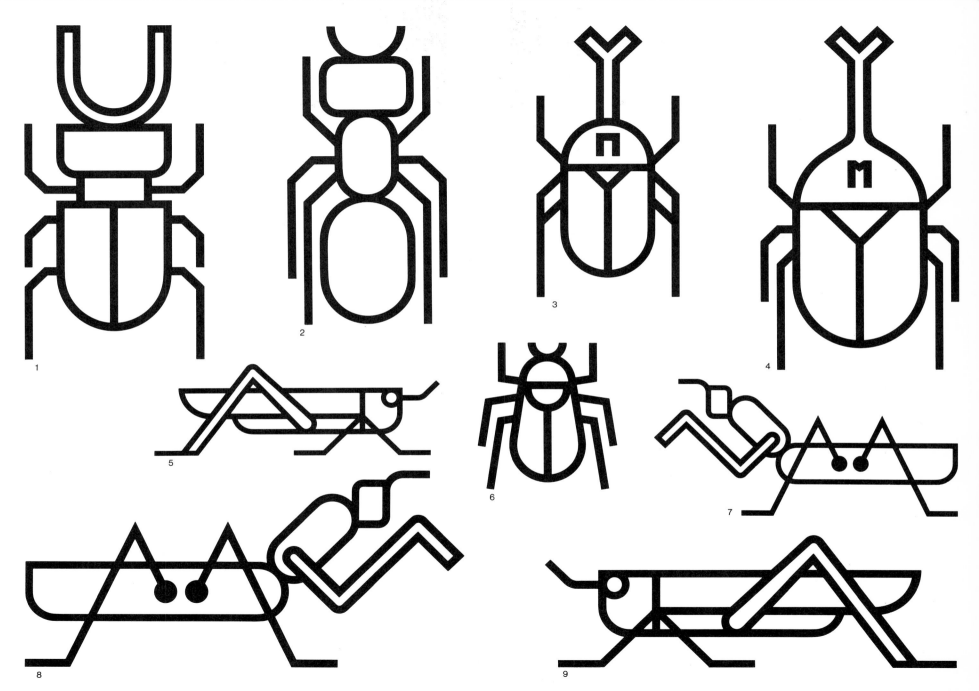

1

2

3

4

5

6

1

2

3

4

5

6

1

2

3

4

5

6

7

8

9

10

11

12

1

2

3

4

5

6

7

8

9

10

11

12

1

2

3

4

5

6

7

8

9

10

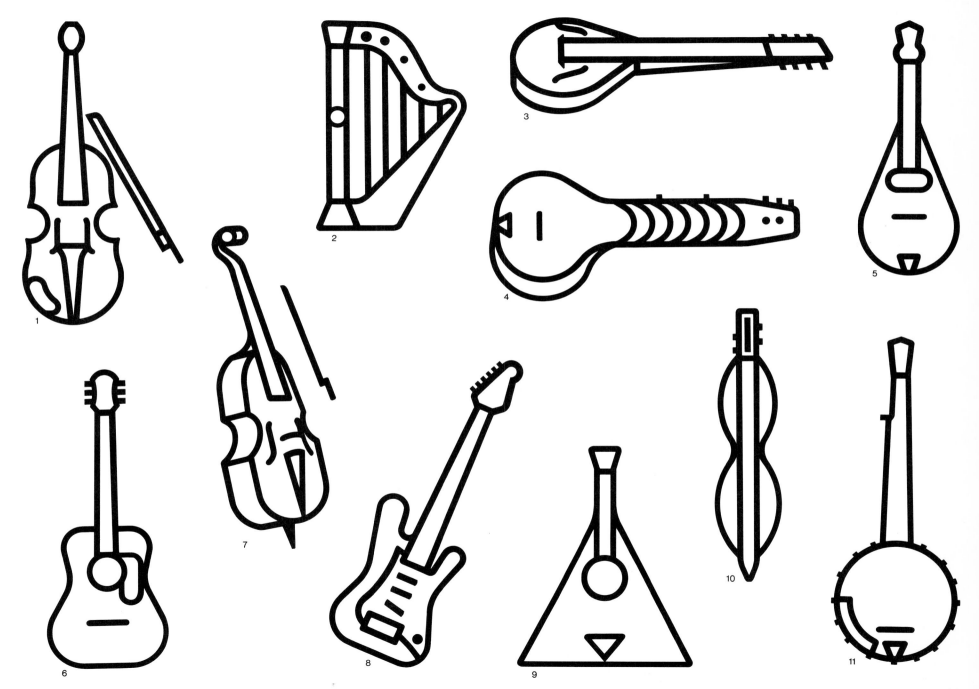

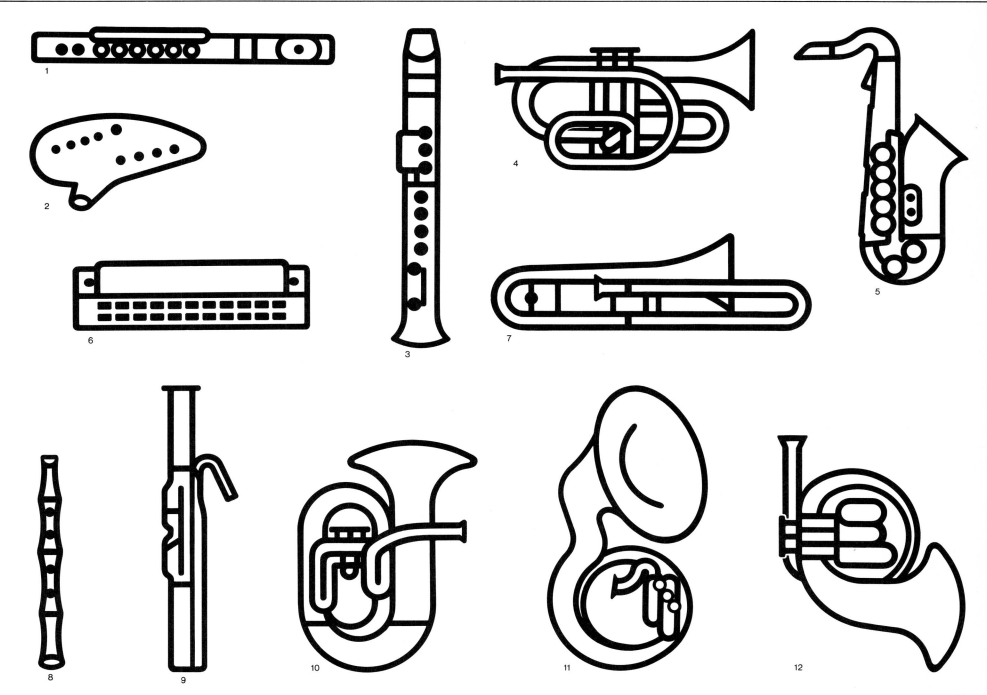

1

2

3

4

5

6

7

8

9

10

11

12

1

2

3

4

5

6

7

8

9

1

2

3

4

5

6

7

8

9

10

11

12

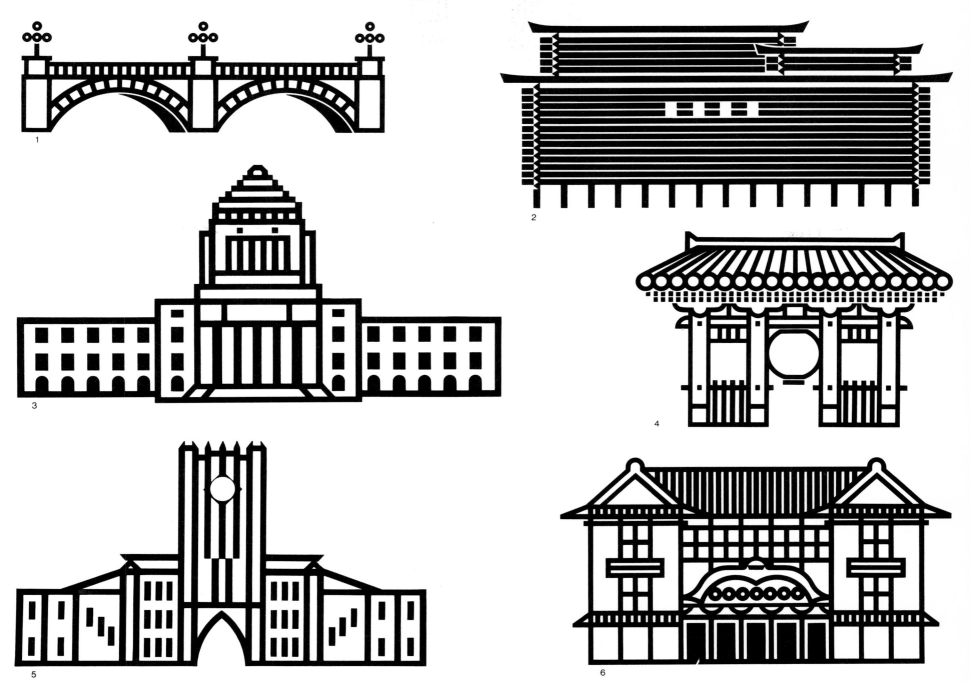

1

2

3

4

5

6

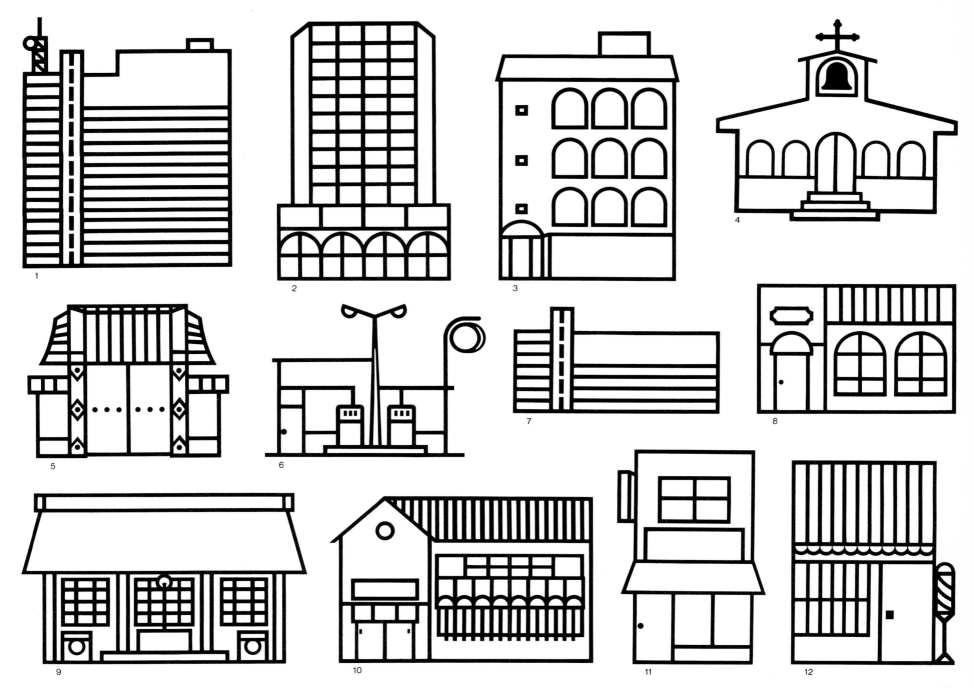

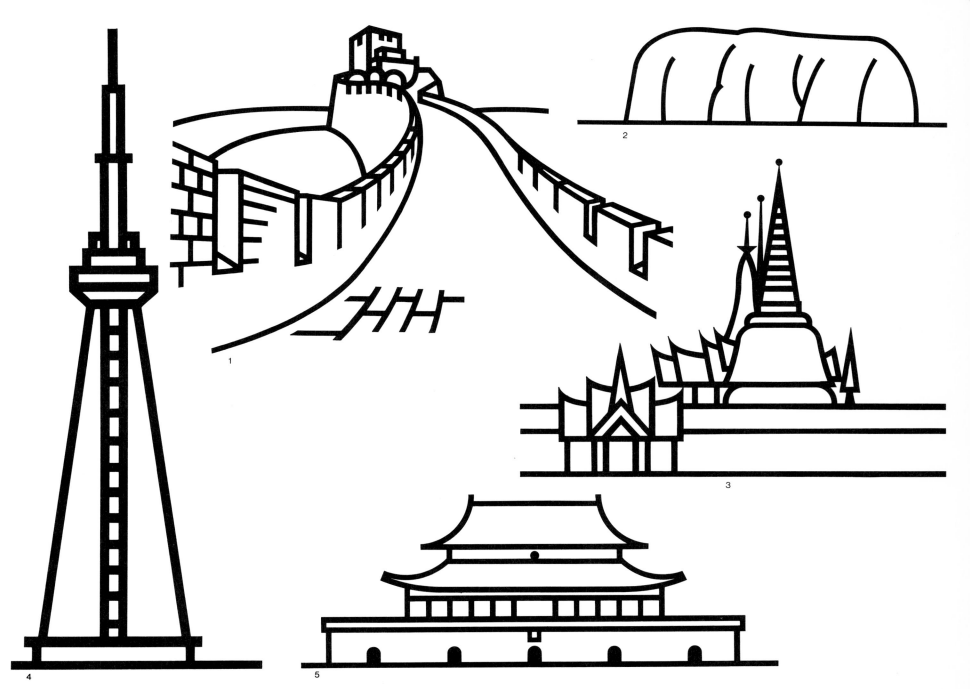

1

2

3

4

5

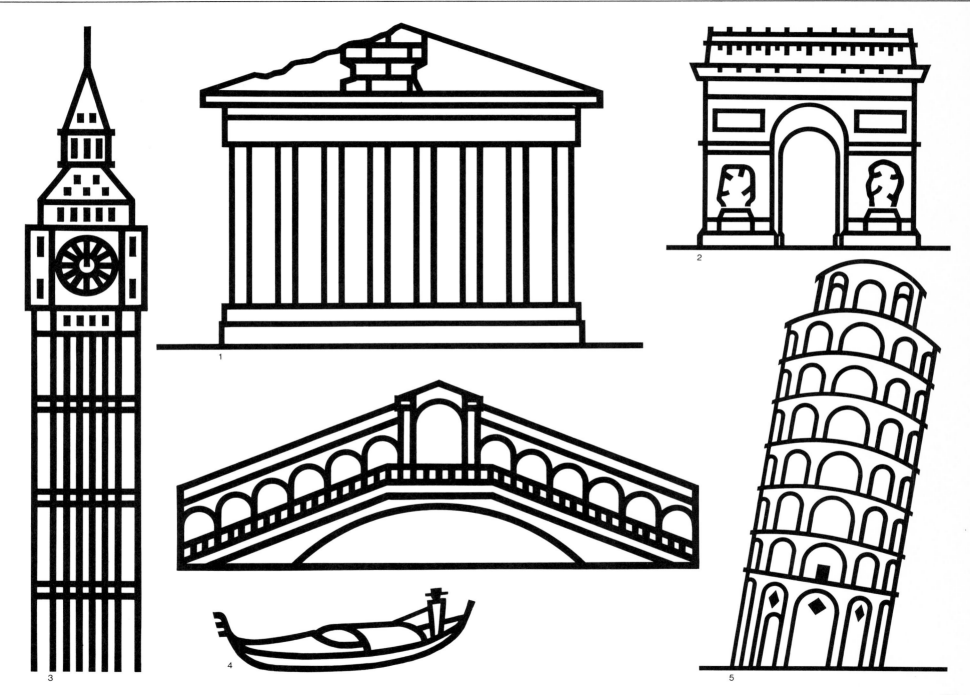

1

3

4

5

6

7

8

9

1

2

3

4

5

6

7

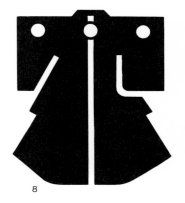

8

9

10

11

12

1

2

3

4

5

6

7

8

9

10

11

12

1

2

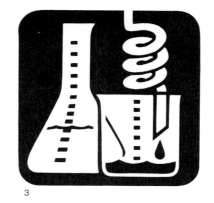

3

4

5

6

7

8

9

10

11

12

1

2

3

4

5

6

7

8

9

10

11

12